The Tarot Trumps
and the
Holy Grail

Great Secrets of the Middle Ages

Margaret Starbird

WovenWord Press

For information write:
WovenWord Press
811 Mapleton Avenue
Boulder, Colorado 80304

Cover Design © 2000 by Vicki McVey

ISBN: 0967842808

Library of Congress Catalogue Card Number 00-106389
1. Religion 2. Spirituality

The Tarot Trumps and the Holy Grail
Great Secrets of the Middle Ages
Margaret Starbird

Grateful acknowledgment to Brian Innes for permission to reproduce the Gringonneur Trumps, Mantegna's "Forteza," and the
Guildhall "cups" emblem from *The Tarot, How to Use and Interpret
the Cards*, London: Macdonald & Co., Ltd., 1976; also to The Paper
Publications Society for permission to reproduce selected watermarks from *The New Briquet Jubilee Edition*, C.M. Briquet, The Paper
Publications Society, 1968.

For Ted
whose strong encouragement
is the rock beneath my feet

ACKNOWLEDGMENTS

Without the staunch support and assistance of my husband, this book would not be. I wish to thank also my very generous father and enthusiastic children for their continued interest in furthering my passion to reclaim the lost Bride in the Christian story. Their support has been an inexhaustible well of encouragement.

I am grateful to Brian Innes, author of *The Tarot, How to Use and Interpret the Cards*, for permitting me to copy the trump cards of the Gringonneur deck and two other images from his personal collection. Additionally, I would like to gratefully acknowledge the permission granted by the Paper Publications Society to render in drawings the medieval watermarks collected by Charles-Moïse Briquet published in their 1968 "Jubilee Edition" of his monumental work *Les Filigranes*. This detailed historical catalogue of medieval watermarks from 1282 –1600 has been invaluable in my research of the "great secrets of the Middle Ages."

For their valued assistance in publishing this book, I thank Sheila Durkin Dierks and Vicki McVey. Their expertise, patience, and skillful handling of the manuscript have been infinitely helpful in seeing the project to completion.

My thanks also to those who read my two earlier books and wrote to express their encouragement for my journey in search of the "Sacred Feminine" in Christianity—so long denied, but blessedly incarnate in Mary, called "the Magdalene." She is to me model, mentor and friend. This little book is offered "in memory of her."

The line drawings of the Visconti-Sforza cups emblem and the "Forteza" card from the Mantegna deck as well as the sixteen images of the Gringonneur tarot trumps are reprinted from *The Tarot, How to Use and Interpret the Cards*, 1976, and appear courtesy of the author, Brian Innes. Two of the images of medieval watermarks, the "IC-88" emblem in figure 2 and the joker in figure 5, are derived from images collected by Harold Bayley, first published in *The Lost Language of Symbolism* in 1912. The remaining watermark illustrations were derived from drawings found in *Les Filigranes* by Charles-Moïse Briquet, in *The New Briquet Jubilee Edition*, 1968, and are used by the kind permission of The Paper Publications Society, Amsterdam. Drawings of the "grail" and mermaid from stone tablets found in Metz (Alsace-Lorraine) are derived from the author's own photographs of these medieval artifacts.

TABLE OF CONTENTS

ILLUSTRATIONS

Tarot Cards

PREFACE

Just before Christmas in 1986 I found myself browsing at the sale table in a local bookstore. My attention was suddenly riveted to the cover of an oversized book featuring pictures of swords and chalices, knights and ladies in fine array and other distinctly medieval images. The little pictures were delicately painted in delightful bright colors, charmingly reminiscent of bygone days of glory and romance. Some of the images were trimmed with gold, others had vine motifs, stars, flowers and other familiar symbols. I was enchanted by the pictures, wondering why they seemed familiar, why they whispered to me of the lost Grail I was so passionately researching at the time. I glanced at the title of the book, which was simply *Tarot*.

I felt a sudden chill. Tarot. Wasn't that something dangerous? Wasn't that something that shouldn't interest me at all because the Church frowned on it? How could these images be related to the Holy Grail? Yet clearly they were! My instinctive response had been sudden, but sure.

I knew nothing at all about the Tarot. But I knew a great deal about the Grail. I had been researching the elusive medieval mystery of the Holy Grail for a long time, and the images on the cover of the Tarot book seemed somehow related to the heresy surrounding the lost artifact.

Enchanted by the gilded picture cards and determined to learn more about the intriguing and delightful images that seemed to have come straight from the heart of the Middle Ages, I bought the sale copy of the Tarot book and took it home—a Christmas present for myself. The tarot trumps and the "great secret" they proclaim radically changed my life.

Of all the intriguing enigmas in medieval art, one that has received renewed attention in recent years is the tarot trumps found in various card collections in Western Europe. An aura of danger and mystery has clung to these images for generations, giving rise to numerous theories about their origin and significance. Speculation about the meaning of the trump cards has been rampant and several bizarre theories have become widely accepted in spite of the fact that they have no basis whatever in real evidence. Over a period spanning two centuries, an enormous amount of misinformation has been circulated concerning the origins of the traditional twenty-two images recognized as the tarot trumps.

In this little volume, I hope to correct some interesting but purely speculative and false notions about the origin of the earliest tarot trumps and the nature of the significant information—the *major arcana*—coded in symbol on the faces of these cards. My study of the tarot trumps is based on concrete historical evidence found in the cards themselves, particularly in the fashionable costumes depicted on the cards and in the symbols that are directly and irrefutably related to the "Church of Amor" and the medieval heresy of the Holy Grail. I do not intend to address in any way the use of the cards for divination or guidance, since this use of the cards has nothing to do with the historical evidence concerning their origins. I intend to show that the earliest extant decks of cards containing twenty-two trumps sprang directly from medieval roots in northern Italy and the Languedoc of southern France. The tarot trumps formed a virtual catechism for the suppressed tenets of the alternative Christian church, the "Church of the Holy Grail," whose tenets of faith included the partnership of Christ and his bride, the woman whom the Gospels called "the Magdalene."

Since the Roman Catholic Church attached such stigma to the cards, branding them dangerous and heretical, it has been rare for someone well versed in Scripture to become deeply involved with the tarot trumps. Yet the trump cards of the earliest decks are best interpreted in light of Scripture references to the dynasty of Israel's royal house, the descendants of King David. It is the medieval heresy of the blood royal—the *sang raal*—that gives us startling and significant clues for deciphering the secret meaning of the tarot trumps.

In my study I have included European history and art, medieval literature and legend, Christian doctrine and tradition, and Scripture itself. Associations from these diverse areas have thrown light on the origins and meanings of the tarot trumps and have culminated in this volume which is the expression of my thesis that the trumps are an historical document from the early to mid-fifteenth century used to record the history and tenets of the "Grail Heresy" so brutally suppressed by the Roman Catholic Church.

CHAPTER I

SOURCES OF THE TAROT

The origin of playing cards is obscure, and for this reason, numerous theories have been offered over several centuries, some of them feasible, others bizarre. Despite rampant speculation about their ancient origins, the earliest mention of cards used for gaming in Europe is found in a document dating from between 1328 and 1341. In 1376 a game called *naibbe* was forbidden by decree in Florence, and another mention of cards appears in the writing of a German monk in the following year. Other documents banning the playing of cards along with other gambling are found dating from the last quarter of the fourteenth century. Nearly a century later, a chronicler named Giovanni Covelluzzo stated in his history of Viterbo (published in 1480) that the game of cards was brought to Viterbo in 1379 from the land of the Saracens.[1]

One theory sometimes offered for the origins of playing cards suggests that returning Crusaders brought them to Europe, but this cannot be substantiated. Christians were driven out of the Middle East in 1291, two decades after the failure of the last Crusade; there is not a shred of evidence that Crusaders brought the cards to Europe. No mention of card playing is made in the literature of the time between 1291 and the document of 1328-41, although gaming and throwing dice are specifically mentioned and condemned in various texts during the period.

Gypsies are sometimes credited with having brought the first tarot decks to Europe, but these migrants first arrived in the mid-fifteenth century, and playing cards were already in use a century before their arrival. It is true that the Gypsies adopted the cards very quickly for divination and fortune-telling. The word *Gypsy* is derived from the erroneous belief of medieval Europeans that this swarthy, dark-eyed people had originated in Egypt, although it is now widely accepted that they came from India and the Balkans, an area known as Romany. Perhaps the false connection of the Gypsies with Egypt contributed directly to the later tenuous speculation that the tarot trumps stemmed from the wisdom of Egypt, a view scholars say is in error in spite of the fact that it is widely repeated.

The plausible theory for the derivation of the playing cards in Europe seems to be that they came from Spain, brought there by the Arabs who occupied it for more than six centuries (the eighth to the fourteenth) and whose cultural influence on the adjacent Mediterranean coast of France was strong. The linguistic root of the word for cards is similar in both languages: *naib* in Arabic, *naipes* in Spanish. However, the earliest decks of playing cards did not contain the so-called trump cards; they consisted only of the four royal or court cards (king, queen, knight and page) and runs numbered from one to ten in each suit. The trump cards, called *major arcana*, were added to later decks painted in France and northern Italy in the fifteenth and later centuries.

Playing cards are known in Korea, China and India as well as in Europe, and in all cases the decks are divided into suits, usually eight or four. The card game played with a deck containing four suits may have derived from an ancient game of "Four Kings" played in India, believed to have been a forerunner of the game of chess as well, and may have been known also to the Gypsies at an early date.

The symbols for the four suits in modern decks found in Germany are not closely related, but the four suits' symbols found in southern European decks are the fore-runners of those familiar in America, Holland and Great Britain today: Spades, Hearts, Diamonds and Clubs. In the earliest French and Italian decks they were called Swords, Chalices, Discs (Coins or Pentacles) and Batons (Scepters). It is the names and symbols for these four suits that are the first strong indicator of their direct relationship to the medieval heresy of the Holy Grail. All four suits of the handsome, vividly hand-painted fifteenth-century decks produced in Provence and northern Italy were clearly associated with the medieval heresy surrounding the surviving descendants of the Holy Grail.

The "Grail heresy" associated with the surviving bloodline of Jesus has received a great deal of attention during the past several decades. Tenets of this alternative view of Christianity claim that the blood royal—

the *sang raal*—of Israel's kings was brought to the
Mediterranean coast of France by Mary Magdalene. The
popular medieval legend asserts that this Mary from the
Gospels traveled with Martha, Lazarus, and several of
their friends, fleeing persecution in Palestine. According
to French legends that are an early source of the Grail
myths, these first-generation Christians washed ashore
in a boat with no oars in A.D. 42 and settled near the
Mediterranean coast of Gaul, the Roman province.

Medieval legends and stories about the Holy Grail
seem to have strong connections with the symbols
found in the tarot decks. They mention several sacred
articles called the Grail Hallows that are connected to
the passion of Jesus Christ: the crown of thorns, the
spear of Longinus that pierced the side of Our Lord,
and the chalice or Grail that caught and contained the
blood flowing from the fatal spear wound. These
ancient symbols of the sword and the cup are not con-
fined to the tarot and the Gospel story; they are repre-
sentations of the masculine and feminine archetypes:
the chalice and the blade. Both symbols are found in an
endless stream in the myths and folklore of peoples
around the globe, including the Celtic Cauldron of
Dagda and the Sword of Nuada that may well have
influenced the early Grail legends of Western Europe.

Widely circulated in the Middle Ages, the legend of
the Holy Grail suggests that the lost artifact was the
chalice used by Christ to establish the Holy Eucharist
at the Last Supper and that Joseph of Arimathea used
the same sacred cup at Golgotha to catch the blood
flowing from the wounded side of the dying savior. In
graphic detail, this legend survives in paintings by
several medieval artists. The underlying kernel of
truth inherent in these legends is that the Grail is a holy

vessel that once contained the blood of Christ. Recent research into the mystery of the Grail shrouded in symbol reveals that the sacred container that once held the blood of Christ was perhaps not an artifact at all, but rather an "earthen vessel." It is my own opinion that the Grail legends refer to a woman—the wife of Jesus, the "vessel" who once contained "the blood of Christ" and brought the blood royal, the *sang raal*, to France.[2] One does not carry the royal bloodline in a jar with a lid. If my interpretation of the medieval French legend is correct, the royal bloodline was carried in a child descended from Jesus and from the royal dynasty of Israel's King David. The feminine symbol of the chalice or Grail might refer to any carrier or container of the royal bloodline—either a mother or a daughter.

CUPS OR CHALICES

The emblem of cups used as one of the suits of cards in medieval tarot decks seems to me to hark directly to the Grail heresy. The very elaborate cup symbol found on some of the early fifteenth-century decks—the Visconti-Sforza packs named for the artist's patrons—is very similar to numerous medieval images of the Holy Grail. And it is precisely the noble families of Provence and northern Italy, the allied ducal families of Anjou and of Milan who were connected by ties of friendship and even related by blood or marriage to the *sang raal*.[3] The trump cards in the fifteenth-century tarot decks belonging to the Visconti family of Milan appear to be among the earliest in existence, from which painters of later decks drew their archetypes and symbols.

The widespread use of a cup or clay vessel as a symbol for the human person is very old. Hebrew

Scriptures include several references to the metaphor of the Potter's vessels as human beings, and Eliakim's descendants are described as "dishes, bowls and jugs" (Isa. 22:24). Saint Paul uses the same metaphor in his epistle: "We have this treasure in earthen vessels" (2 Cor. 4:7). Human beings are indeed "sacred containers" of the gift of life. The fancy Grail-chalices on the cards of the cups suit and elsewhere in medieval art, with their elaborate tiers and turrets, often look more like castles than chalices.

"Cups" Suit emblem

This connection of the Grail with a "stronghold" or "walled city" will become clearer presently when we discuss the images on the actual tarot trumps. The cup suit of the tarot seems carefully crafted to represent the feminine chalice—the archetypal "sacred container." And, of course, the "feminine" is specifically the container for a bloodline—the *sang raal*—with which the Grail heresy is linked. In particular, the Visconti family of Milan was proud of its connections by marriage with the royal house of England, the Plantagenets.

Figure 1. "Grail" or Cup[4]

SWORDS

The suit of swords has been widely believed to represent the knights or class of the nobles or peers of Europe. Its archetypal significance as the symbol for masculine energy is well researched and documented. In early decks, the swords pictured were unmistakable, a symbol representing the masculine "blade" *(lingam)* in juxtaposition with the feminine "chalice" *(yoni)*. The stylized ♠ used in modern card decks bears a strong resemblance to the spike of the fleur-de-lis *(iris germanicus)*. This device is often called the "little sword" and is the heraldic emblem of the royal Merovingians so intimately connected with the heresy of the "blood royal." It is commonly associated with the French royal dynasties and with France itself.

BATONS or SCEPTERS

In early card decks, the suit of clubs or batons was often pictured as a flowering staff, similar to the staff often held by a king in medieval art, usually with a stylized fleur-de-lis on the head. I believe this emblem is specifically connected with the Merovingian bloodline in Europe. In the Hebrew Bible, and in Christian legend, the symbol of the budding staff implies that a person is chosen by God for a special role. Modern day statues of Saint Joseph, the husband of Mary, show him holding a flowering staff, derived from a legend which I believe directly alludes to the biblical prophecies concerning the princely bloodline of Judah and the budding staff of Jesse. The expected messiah of Israel was traditionally called both the "scepter" (from Gn. 49:10) and the "shoot" (Zec. 3:8) from the "root of Jesse" (Is. 11:1), metaphors referring to his Davidic descent. He is called "the Scepter" in the War Scroll found among the Dead Sea Scrolls hidden in jars near Qumran. Among the Grail heretics, a scepter or staff that is budding or flowering seems to have been adopted as an appropriate symbol for the messiah and his descendants. If this interpretation is correct, then the budding staff suit of the card decks represented the royal legacy of the bloodline of the Grail family descended from the shepherd-king David, the youngest son of Jesse (1 Sm. 1:16) and from Jesus Christ who is called "Son of David" in the Gospels.

Medieval artists delighted in representing the human genealogy of Jesus on a family tree beginning with Jesse, usually found asleep at the root of the great tree growing from his side. One famous Jesse Tree is rendered in stained glass in Our Lady's Cathedral at Chartres, its jewel-like fragments forming a fabulous mosaic showing the ancestors of Christ through ten centuries of Jewish history. Both the Gospel of Matthew and that of Luke provide genealogies of Jesus through

Saint Joseph all the way back to King David (although they differ in the names of the ancestors!). Saint Paul, in his letter to the Romans, mentions that Jesus is descended from David "according to the flesh." It seems that this became a favorite theme of the Middle Ages, the Kingship of Jesus derived from his royal lineage, a theme articulated in the "budding staff" of the club suit.

COINS, PENTACLES AND DIAMONDS

Today's diamond suit was derived from earlier decks in which the suit appears as a five-pointed star. The pentacle was a symbol for the planet Venus, named for the love goddess of Roman antiquity. Every eight years the orbit of the planet Venus sketches a perfect pentacle around the sun, so the ☆ and the number five have long been associated with the planet Venus in her unique relationship to the sun.[5]

The number eight had very special significance for Christians. Very early in the Christian community, Jesus Christ was known as the 888 (the *gematria* of IHSOUS using traditional numerical values for the Greek letters) and identified with the number 8 which, in their canon of sacred numbers, bore the symbolic significance of "resurrection," "renewal" and the "dawn of the new day."[6] Jesus had been raised on the eighth day—the day after the Sabbath or seventh day of the week. He was understood to be the "dawn of the new day." The patriarchs of the early Church called Christ the *Ogdoad*, the "fullness of eights," and also "Sun of our righteousness."

By association with Venus, the ☆ was a symbol for Mary Magdalene, the Christian embodiment of the Goddess of Love, orbiting around her Christ-Sun every eight years. I believe she was the *Dompna* (Provençal for the Latin word *Domina* or Lady) as Christ was their

Dominus—Lord and Lady of the hidden Church of the Grail.

The strong association of the pentacle with Magdalene-Venus and with the alternative Christian Church of Love may have influenced the subsequent evolution of the suit called cups or chalices into the heart suit in current card decks. Like the chalice, the heart is a sacred container. An interesting symbol found among the watermarks of the alternative medieval Church of Love is an emblem containing double eights—88.[7] This symbolic abbreviation of the "888" of Jesus is formed by two hearts intertwined in intimate embrace. Thus the connection between the hearts and the eights is reinforced in the Church of *Amor*, which is itself an anagram and the perceived opposite of the hierarchical and repressive Church of *Roma*.

Figure 2. Iesu Christi—"88"

In discussing the origins of the diamond suit, we must mention its earlier manifestation as a circle in the suit known in the Italian Visconti-Sorfza decks as disks or coins which were often decorated with a flower. No one knows for certain why the suit symbols were chosen, but if my theory is correct, they were all related to the tenets and symbols of the Grail heresy. Like the ☆, the circle is strongly associated with Mary Magdalene. From the sixth century in the West, the feast day of this

"Beloved" of Christ was celebrated on July 22nd , the twenty-second day of the seventh month. These numbers, 7 and 22, are uniquely significant; they represent the ratio known since ancient times as *pi* or π —the ratio of the circumference of a circle to its diameter. So designating the feast day of Mary Magdalene on this date provided an immediate association of this saint with the properties of the circle. In some of the early decks, the suit of coins is represented by a golden disk with a flower in the center, a rose representing the love goddess and the sacred feminine. In addition to her feast day, Mary Magdalene's sacred number by *gematria* is also uniquely connected with the properties of a circle and the specifically with the Vesica Piscis, the () associated with the sacred feminine in ancient times.[8]

Among the outstanding characteristics of the heretical sects of southern France was their passionate love for Scripture and the enthusiasm with which they translated and copied the Gospels. To answer their need, numerous paper mills dating from the late thirteenth century sprang up in the region. An ingenious method for hiding the tenets of their faith was devised: under the malevolent scrutiny of the Inquisition formed in 1233 to squelch the heresies of Provence, watermarks were designed and imbedded in the actual leaves of paper on which the heretics transcribed their Scriptures. These watermarks are elegant symbol-fossils that attest to the unorthodox tenets of their faith. Among these indelible emblems are found numerous allusions to the Grail, the Merovingian fleur-de-lis (called the "little sword"), hearts and 88s, stars and budding staffs related to the suits of cards—all developed during the same historical era and in the same geographic location. We will discuss the watermarks of the "other Church" more thoroughly in connection with the meaning of the individual trumps of the tarot. These fossils are eloquent surviving proof of what I consider the undeniable connection between the heretics and the symbols found in the *major arcana*—the Great Secrets of the tarot.

1. The Emperor

2. The Pope

3. The Lovers

4. The Hermit

5. Strength

6. The Charioteer

7. Justice

8. The Hanged Man

9. Death

10. Prudence

11. The Devil

12. The Tower

13. The Moon

14. The Sun

15. Judgment

16. The World

CHAPTER 2

ORIGINS OF THE TAROT
TRUMPS

We have examined the symbols of the four suits of a deck of cards and their strong symbolic relationship with the heresy of the Holy Grail, without yet discussing the *major arcana*, the tarot trumps. It is with regard to these enigmatic trump cards, traditionally twenty-two in number, that most misinformation has been circulated in recent years.

In his book, *The Tarot, How to Use and Interpret the Cards*, Brian Innes thoroughly debunks the speculation that the tarot trumps survived the ravages and repression of centuries and can be traced directly to the ancient wisdom of Egypt.[1] An obscure Protestant theologian from southern France, Court de Gebelin, is the source of this bogus and extravagant claim first published in 1781 in his book *Monde Primitif.* The author hypothesized archetypal significance for the twenty-two trumps of the tarot deck, based on pure speculation and on the glamorous aura surrounding Egyptian art and artifacts that existed in France at the time. His book was read by a wigmaker in Paris named Alliette, who immediately seized on the ideas of Court de Gebelin and fabricated even more elaborate evidence of the Egyptian origins of the tarot cards, attributing them to a book planned by Hermes Trimegistos, the *Book of Thoth.* De Gebelin was fascinated by the Jewish Kabbalah and ventured to identify the twenty-two trumps with the twenty-two paths connecting the ten *sefiroth* of the mystical Tree of Life.

Leaping upon this novel idea, the French occultist Eliphas Lévi related each tarot trump of the standard deck to one of the twenty-two letters of the Hebrew alphabet. A later disciple of Lévi, choosing the pseudonym of Paul Christian, wrote a treatise called the *History of Magic,* published in Paris in 1860. Herein he described initiation rites of the Egyptian Mysteries and the use of twenty-two paintings along the walls of the Great Pyramid, all the product of his own very vivid imagination! Some who have read these extravagant claims have accepted them without ever questioning their authenticity. I believe the idea that the tarot trumps stem from Egypt is elaborate fable, not fact.

Numerous variations, amplifications and exaggerations of these speculated eighteenth-century themes and motifs sprang up and proliferated in all directions, most based on the Marseilles tarot pack, the eighteenth-century pack originally described in Court de Gebelin's work. The images from the early tarot decks are not in any respect Egyptian and did not derive from any prototype in Egypt. They are demonstrably medieval and European and, in my opinion, are directly related to legends, prophecies, and loosely kept secrets of the suppressed heresy of the Holy Grail and the royal Merovingian bloodline.

Based on factual empirical evidence, the most likely prototype of the trumps is found among the medieval "instructive" cards used as visual aid for memorization of easily recognized images. These systems of colorful images were used to educate in a time when books were expensive and rare.[2] Saints and their symbols were often depicted on such cards, along with biblical and mythological characters from antiquity, personifications of the cardinal sins and virtues, the seven disciplines of knowledge, the seven known planets, the signs of the zodiac and other information memorized by an intellectual of the time. The well-known fifty-card deck erroneously attributed to the Italian painter Mantegna (1431-1506) is an example of an instructive card series of this type.

Another card deck, produced in Florence for the Italian game called *minchiate*, contained forty-two trumps including the twelve signs of the zodiac, the four elements, the four virtues and many of the traditional images repeated in the tarot decks—emperor, empress, pope, hermit and fool, but not the stricken tower or the hanged man, two images that are unique to the tarot decks.

The surviving trump cards of what I believe to be the earliest painted tarot deck—the so-called Gringonneur or

Charles VI deck—were until recently believed to be those mentioned in an account book from the court treasurer of Charles VI of France. The accountant annotated payment in 1392 for three decks of cards to entertain the king, money paid to the artist Jacquemin Gringonneur for "gilded and painted cards in bright colors."

In light of the fashions worn by the figures on the faces of these particular trump cards, it has lately been suggested that these cards probably belong to a slightly later deck of the early fifteenth century originating in Venice rather than those mentioned in the French treasurer's notation.[3] Yet somehow the cards ended up in the estate of an assistant tutor of the grandchildren of Louis XIV and were bequeathed to the French King in 1711. They are now in the possession of the *Biblièteque Nationale* in Paris.

Although the name given the Gringonneur deck is believed to have been an error, the trumps remain, in my opinion, the earliest example of the genre. The costumes worn by the dancing couples depicted on the Lovers card help us to establish the age of the trumps of the Gringonneur deck relative to that of extant trumps from various other decks. Specifically, the high headdress with the exaggerated letter "M" is reminiscent of elaborate fourteenth-century *escoffion* worn by noble and wealthy ladies in southern Europe. A statuette dating from the early fifteenth century in Amsterdam depicts a Dutch countess wearing a "split-loaf," heart-shaped headdress fastened to an embroidered *caul* similar to the one worn by the central woman "lover." The tights and short jackets of the male dancers were in vogue at about the turn of the century, as was the padded coat of the Page of Swords from the Gringonneur deck with its "vine" pattern, a distinctive motif of the trumps from this significant tarot deck. Costumes from the so-called Visconti-Sforza decks seem to indicate a slightly later date.

The Gringonneur deck contains, I believe, the oldest extant examples of tarot trumps. In addition to the evidence provided by the costumes is the fact that the trumps are not named and have no numbers on them, a possible indicator that they were a prototype of the class known as "tarot trumps" but painted before the order of the trumps became fixed by later copyists. Additionally, the cards that are most enigmatic when compared to the instructive or memory cards of the period, are precisely the cards most closely linked to the tenets of the Grail heresy: The Popess, the Hanged Man, the Stricken Tower and Judgment Day.

The Gringonneur deck retains sixteen of its original trump cards and one face card, the Page or Knave of Swords. These cards are less sophisticated than those of the Visconti-Sorfza decks usually dated between 1440-1480. I believe that the symbols on the Gringonneur trumps are purer and therefore earlier than those of the other tarot decks in question. One probable indicator of this theory is the vine motif found in the background of the Gringonneur cards that in the Visconti decks has been replaced by a background of Xs. Because of the association of the vine with the blood royal of the descendents of the "Vine of Judah," I believe the vine to be the earlier motif. Certain emblems connected with the Visconti family coat-of-arms do not occur at all in the Gringonneur trumps, indicating that the latter were painted for a different, probably earlier, patron.

I hope to provide evidence that the symbols on these earliest trumps relate specifically to the medieval Grail heresy.[4] And for that reason it is specifically the Gringonneur trumps that need to be examined for the historical fossils of the heresy for which they provided a visual catechism or series of instructive memory cards. Centuries of revision and re-interpretation of the tarot trumps by later artists have resulted in literally hundreds of decks derived from the earliest traditional images. The purity of the early Gringonneur (Charles VI) images most clearly demonstrates their relationship to the Grail heresy of the "Church of Love," and so we turn now to this deck to decipher the Great Secrets of the Middle Ages, the *major arcana.*

CHAPTER 3

THE TROMPES

hat are the tarot trumps? The origin of the word is the Old French *trompe* meaning "trumpet." Its Latin root is related to trumpets and their heralding of triumph. Even today, in our modern games, to "trump" is to win the trick—literally to triumph.

The trumps in the early tarot decks were understood from their inception to be heretical. They were not considered dangerous merely because gaming was declared sinful by the hierarchy of the Roman Catholic Church, but rather, because the cards themselves were known to contain information that was heretical. In the popular French epic poem, *The Song of Roland*, widely circulated in the Middle Ages, the trumpet blast of the hero split the rocks of the Pyrenees when he signaled for help. Roland, a nephew of the Franks' king Charlemagne, died a hero and martyr in the battle to save France from the onslaught of the Moors, and the final trumpet blast on his "Oliphant" was legendary! In cryptic medieval jargon, heretical preaching of the true Gospel was seen as a trumpet that could split the "rock" of Peter's Church. And the tarot *trompes* were just such powerful heretical trumpets. Among the watermarks of the heretics we find numerous emblems depicting a trumpet in this light.

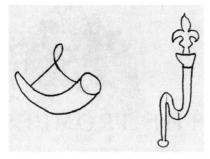

Figure 3. Trumpets

A monk in the mid-fifteenth century warned of the danger inherent in the images of the tarot trumps, describing them as "rungs on a ladder that leads straight to the depths of hell."[1] Beyond the condemnation of gaming in general, the cards were understood to be heretical and therefore dangerous, but interpreters of the cards cannot explain why that impassioned view was so widespread. What great secret was coded in the images on the cards that could be powerful enough to split the rock of the Roman Catholic establishment?

I believe that close scrutiny of the individual cards and their relationship to the heresy of the Grail holds the key to their correct interpretation. We will examine the trumps of the Gringonneur tarot deck in their traditionally accepted order, although the cards of this early deck were not numbered.

THE FOOL

Later decks that used the standard twenty-two images begin with a card marked with a "0," which they name The Fool, a card that is no longer extant in the deck we are examining, but which still exists in many other decks. The Fool is the seeker, the Parsifal figure, the one not yet initiated into the secrets of the heresy. In the watermarks of the heretics, he is often blindfolded. He stumbles into the quest almost by accident. He is a nobody, a "zero." But the 0 is called *l'oeuf* (the egg) in French, a word connected phonetically with the English "love," as we know from keeping score in the game of tennis where a score of "0" *(l'oeuf)* is called "love." This same egg is a symbol for new life and spiritual rebirth through enlightenment. It has endless potential.

The fool or simpleton is an archetype. He is on a journey to learn the truth and must ask questions along the way. Other early tarot packs present the Fool as an itinerant beggar, his faithful dog at his heels. Since the dog in medieval art is often a symbol for its English anagram, it represents the "presence of God" in iconography. The wise fool is ubiquitous in fairytale, often rewarded for an altruistic good or daring deed he performs—a gratuitous act of kindness. "We are fools for Christ" is a slogan of the Albigensian preachers of the Gospel who traveled in pairs, working in the fields side-by-side with the peasants of Provence, sharing their bread and propagating the Word of God.[2] "We hunger and thirst, we are naked and buffeted, and we have no fixed abode. We are reviled, and we bless, are persecuted and we bear with it" (1 Cor. 4:10). These fools for Christ were the "pure ones" *(cathari)*—the itinerant preachers of the Cathar heresy so ruthlessly suppressed by the Inquisition and mercenary armies of pope and king during the bitter years of the brutal Albigensian crusade (1209-1250).

THE JOKER

The second trump card, also unfortunately missing from the Gringonneur deck, is now known as The Adept or Magician, but in some early decks he was called The Juggler. He is the initiated one, the one who knows the secrets. He is the artisan or trickster in the tradition of Hermes, the messenger of the gods noted for his subtlety. These jugglers and acrobats were the clowns of God.

Figure 4. Clown

Touring troupes of jugglers, jokers and jongleurs (troubadours) are reliably credited with having disseminated the suppressed secrets of the hidden alternative Christianity throughout Europe, traveling from court to court and town to town with the subversive message of their secret Gospel.[3] This trump card survives in our modern decks as a joker, with his peaked cap and pointed shoes, the most revolutionary character in the human family. He uses humor to reveal truth. Even in today's card games, the joker wins all! The joker reminds us of the court jester, whose role it was to make even the king look ridiculous. He is anti-establishment and turns the tables on the established order with his jibes. Images similar to the jokers in our current decks of cards appear among the heretical watermarks collected and catalogued from the pages of medieval Bibles.[4]

The true adept in the spiritual realm is one who is enlightened by the Holy Spirit because of his dedication to the "Way" of the heart. He serves willingly, seeks the wisdom of God and understands the hermetic secret of synchronicity that provides a flash of inspiration in the tradition of Hermes, the god of the crossroads. Joker watermarks often include the number four, symbolic of the "crossroad" principle of synchronicity, the uncanny coincidence of mind and matter that so often brings instant enlightenment.

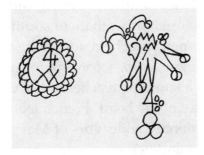

Figure 5. Joker, Hermetic "4"

The joker in modern card decks seems to be a composite of the first two trump cards—the fool and the adept. Several significant features in the joker emblems should be noted. First, his costume displays M's—possibly connected with Mary Magdalene and her "Way of Love"—and also little circles cut in half. This symbol, frequent in medieval art, represents the *conjunctio* of the sun and moon—the sacred union which is the symbol for symmetry and balance of the opposites—the yin/yang principle of Chinese philosophy. The adept and the juggler rely on perfect balance and timing for the practice of their art.

THE PAPESS

The next card, the Female Pope or Papess, although missing from the Gringonneur pack, probably resembled the image in the trump series of later decks. In keeping with the egalitarian principles of the Gospel they embraced, a female spiritual teacher or priestess is here acknowledged as Papess of their alternative Christianity, in juxtaposition with the Pope of the Petrine tradition pictured in card numbered five. Although the Roman Catholic Church did not allow women to be priests, the Cathars of southern France encouraged women preachers, following the tradition of Mary Magdalene, who, according to strong Gnostic traditions, was a supreme teacher of the Christian "Way"—the Way of the heart. French legends confirmed the missionary endeavors of Mary Magdalene in southern France and her grave was fortuitously rediscovered near Marseilles in 1279, reinforcing the popular folklore surrounding her in that region. Ostensibly, the gravesite had been moved to protect it from possible desecration by invading Moors of the eighth century.

Among medieval paintings of Mary Magdalene, one painted by the Flemish "Master of the Magdalene Legend" shows her preaching the Gospel to townspeople gathered in a forest to hear her words. Of course, she could not preach to them from a podium in a Catholic Church, but only out in the open fields and forests, where the credants of the heretical protestant sects of the Middle Ages so often flocked to meet their preachers in secret and under cover of darkness.

In the Bempo deck of 1484, the Papess is carrying a book, symbol for Wisdom. "Wisdom" is female in the Hebrew Scriptures, the beloved bride of Yahweh. In a wonderful metaphor, she hawks her wares in the streets, but only rarely is anyone interested. Like the feminine principle itself, wisdom is too often ignored, reviled and scorned. Only the enlightened seek her precepts. She is the personification of the Wisdom of God and the Jewish Torah—the Law.

The Gnostic Christians extolled Wisdom as the "Beloved of Christ" incarnate in Mary Magdalene. According to the Gnostic Gospel of Philip discovered at Nag Hammadi, she was the favorite of Christ, his "consort" and constant companion, whom he often kissed upon the mouth.[5] Wisdom was one of the significant attributes often associated with Mary Magdalene from the very earliest days of the Church, when exegetes of Scripture often equated her with the Holy Sophia as well as the beloved Sister-Bride from the Song of Solomon. Among the Gnostics whose library was found at Nag Hammadi, Mary Magdalene was known as "the woman who knew the All," who received secret teachings from Jesus that were not imparted to the apostles. In their alternative version of Christianity, Mary Magdalene was the pre-eminent disciple and teacher of Christ's Gospel, the "Apostle to the Apostles."

25

The Papess of the tarot represents the doctrines and spirit of the "other" Christian church of the High Middle Ages—the Church that valued the Gnostic path of personal enlightenment and honored the sacred feminine principle of Holy Wisdom incarnate in Mary Magdalene.

THE EMPRESS

The next trump card pictures The Empress, also sadly missing from the Gringonneur deck. Her image, like that of her masculine counterpart, traditionally appears in the earlier memory decks. She represents the archetype of temporal power vested in a female ruler. In the Bempo deck she bears a shield with the emblem of an eagle (or possibly a Phoenix, the mythological bird resurrected from the ashes). Often her elaborate gown bears embroidered images of flowering vines and crowns suitable to her royal status and very similar to gowns worn by Mary Magdalene in numerous medieval paintings. This gold brocade is significant. According to Psalm 45, "The Nuptial Ode of the Messianic King," gold brocade is the raiment of the bride of the reigning sovereign: "All glorious is the king's daughter as she enters; her raiment is threaded with spun gold. In embroidered apparel she is borne in to the king." Since ancient times, the robe of the royal bride has been threaded with gold, and in countless medieval paintings, Mary Magdalene is robed in a similar fashion.

THE EMPEROR

The King or Emperor is pictured in the next card, the temporal ruler of the domain. The Emperor is the first trump card in the traditional sequence that has survived in the Gringonneur pack. He holds the scepter and orb of his exalted office and two pages kneel beside his throne. The usual number given this trump is four, which is ironic if these trumps were, as I believe, a catechism of the Grail faith. For it was the French King Philip IV who destroyed the Order of the Knights of the Temple of Solomon, the Templars who were the medieval protectors of the Grail family and its secrets. And it was in collaboration with Pope Clement V that Philip IV was able to arrest the Templars simultaneously in all the cities of France and have them tortured and executed under trumped-up charges of blasphemy. If these cards were meant to tell the story of the Church of the Holy Grail, then the cards numbered four and five are an integral part of the history.

THE POPE

Is it accidental that the card bearing the image of the Pope is numbered five? I believe this number might be a surreptitious reference to the ignominious Pope Clement V, a clever mnemonic device to aid in the memorization of the story depicted in the cards. Pope Clement was the puppet of Philip IV, who moved him to Avignon in 1305 to begin the French exile of the papacy known as the "Babylonian Captivity." We will meet these temporal rulers—Pope and Emperor—again, on the face of the card called Death. But the image also represents the pope as leader of the Church of Peter, the Church of Rome. Here in the fifth card, two cardinals dressed in red cassocks attend the pope, who holds a key, presumably the key given by Jesus to Saint Peter, the key to the kingdom.

But originally, according to the Gospel, there were "keys" to the kingdom—more than one key (Mt. 16:19). Is it possible, or even likely, that the Papess on the earlier card—now lost—was bearer of the other key? Perhaps that is why her image no longer exists. Perhaps she was expunged because of the suggestion that she held the other key to salvation—the secret knowledge of the esoteric Gnostic tradition and of the "sacred feminine" as true partner.

Figure 6. Keys

Luke's Gospel tells us an interesting story that is relevant to the pictorial evidence in the Tarot. In Lk. 5:5-7, Jesus tells Peter, who has fished all night without success, to lower his nets. The subsequent catch of fishes is so enormous that Peter calls the boat of his friends, John and James, to help with bringing the fishes ashore. In the accepted metaphor of the New Testament, the "fishes in the net" are the converts to Christianity, the "Church" herself. So, in the understanding of the heretics, Peter's boat (the Roman Catholic Church) was not sufficient to harvest the entire catch, but required the help of the "other boat" to bring in the marvelous catch of fishes.

Were these heretics not (metaphorically speaking) the fishermen in the "other boat"—the "boat of John?" In their eyes, the "fishes" of the Christian message could not be harvested by "Peter's bark" alone. They identified strongly with the Beloved disciple, the one whom Jesus loved mentioned in the Gospel of John. Their help was urgently needed for the successful evangelization to the "Way" of Christ. They held the "other key"—the understanding of the sacred feminine at the heart of the Christian story.

THE LOVERS

Following the Pope's card is the trump traditionally called The Lovers. I believe this card might easily be named The Vine. The clues linking it to the Grail heresy are remarkable for their clarity. The lovers pictured are in pairs, dancing in a line, dressed in the attire of the court, nobles and their ladies—the peers of Europe. The woman dancer in the middle is wearing a headdress with an exaggerated blue M framing her face, a style that reached the popular peak of fashion in the first decades of the fifteenth century. The dancers are clapping their hands and singing. Above them are two cupid-like angels, their arrows aimed at the lovers, each cupid sporting a red X across its breast.

The letter X, and explicitly a red X, was a significant identifying symbol of the heretical church, discussed at length in my book, *The Woman with the Alabaster Jar*.[6] Numerous Xs have been found in caves used as Cathar hideouts during the ruthless thirteenth century crusade against them. The X was a rebus formed from the combination of the stylized *L*, *V*, and *X* spelling *lux*, the Latin word for light. The letter *X* is also seen to contain the first two letters, Λ and *V*, which in symbolic language represent the masculine and feminine energies, the blade and the chalice. The heretics used the letter *X* standing

29

alone to represent enlightenment, (*lux* in Latin), an ingenious symbol for the fundamental tenet of their faith. It is interesting to note that the watermarks manufactured by the heretics and hidden in the pages of their medieval Bibles were only visible when the pages were held up to the LIGHT. Theirs was a Gnostic or "moist" (green!) spirituality of enlightenment through personal encounter with God, in marked contrast to the "dry" traditions of the Church of indoctrination and legalism—the Church of Rome.

Another symbol often found among the watermarks of the medieval heretics was the palm of the hand. Its symbolic meaning was "hold to the true faith"—a word of encouragement to those undergoing trials and oppression at the hands of the Inquisition. It is particularly significant in connection with the heresy of the royal bloodline of Judah, because a Roman symbol for the nation of Israel was the palm tree, found minted on coins during the Roman occupation of Israel. The palm is *phoenix* in Greek, associated with the fantastic mythical bird that rises whole from his own ashes, a particularly poignant symbol for Christ and the hope of his return. Two of the dancers on the Lovers card are displaying a palm, the symbol of hope and encouragement to those who share the Great Secret.

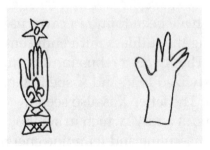

Figure 7. Palms

The dancers-lovers in this card represent the bloodline of the Grail, the "Vine of the line of Judah." As mentioned earlier, all the trump cards of the Gringonneur deck have a graceful vine motif decorating the blank areas in the background, and the clapping and singing dancers seem to be celebrating the "fruit of the vine." In this deck, the surviving court card depicts a knight with a padded coat embroidered with a vine motif as well. Medieval descendants of the Merovingian bloodline seem to have called themselves "the Vine," a distinct reference to the Vine of Judah: "Israel is the vineyard of the Lord, and the men of Judah are his cherished plant"(Is. 5:7); and also of Jesus: "I am the vine" (Jn. 15:5). The M-headdress of the central female dancer on the card could easily refer to the Merovingian dynasty—literally the "vine of Mary." The kings of the Merovingian dynasty were traditionally buried with their swords and with a collection of little golden bees, a symbol representing their royal matriarch. Their seat of power was at Metz in Lorraine, a town whose name was derived from the earlier Roman city that occupied the same site at the confluence of two rivers—a city originally known as Mediomatrix—the "mother-center." The royal matriarch of their dynasty was allegedly the Mary called "the Magdalene"—the "other" Mary.

On a recent trip to Metz, I discovered several very surprising stone artifacts that once decorated the little church, Saint Peter to the Nuns, one of the earliest Christian churches built in the Roman province of Gaul. Grail and vine motifs very similar to those found among the watermarks were carved into tablets of stone dating from the sixth or seventh century, the peak of the Merovingian era. And among the tablets was one of a double-tailed mermaid with a vine of Merovingian

31

fleur-de-lis entwined around her. This mermaid image, numerous among the watermarks of medieval Bibles, is now ubiquitous in the Starbuck's emblem posted on coffee houses world-wide!

Drawing of the Mermaid from stone tablet at Metz

A peculiar legend has clung to this vine for centuries. Based on ancient folklore, it is whispered that the royal Merovingians were descended from a mermaid, and from a king Merovée whose ancestry was "half man, half fish." This legend has interesting implications when we remember that Christ was so often called the ICHTHYS (the fish) and that the *gematria* for the Magdalene identifies this special Mary with the *Vesica Piscis*—the () known as the "vessel of the fish."[7] Perhaps these Beloveds were recognized as the Lord and Lady of Pisces, the "Age to Come," and their descendants thus acknowledged.

Among the artifacts I discovered in a museum in the heart of Lorraine was an antique board with a painted image of a fish that bore the bearded face of Jesus and was linked to an image of a mermaid with a double tail. The images were a startling illustration of the Merovingian myth of their ancestral couple,"the fishes." Many of the mermaids found among the watermarks bear a mirror, a symbol commonly associated with the Love Goddess, not because she is vain, but because she represents "matter" as the mirror of divinity. The mermaid is a diminutive reminder of the Great Goddess as Queen of the Sea.

Figure 8. Mermaids

THE HERMIT

The card that bears the number seven in later decks is The Charioteer, but here I believe the numbering system is corrupted. As I have already mentioned, the trumps of the very early Gringonneur deck have no numbers; these were added only on later decks. For historical reasons I believe that the seventh card should be called The Hermit and that The Charioteer should be switched to appear later in the sequence, becoming the number nine card.

The Hermit pictured on this card is Peter the Hermit, the zealous monk who preached the First Crusade throughout the cities of Europe in 1080-95, calling upon the knights to gather their retainers and travel to the Middle East to liberate the Holy City Jerusalem from the Saracens. Peter the Hermit is an historical figure in the political arena, and his apparent agenda was to place a scion from the Merovingian bloodline on the throne of David in Jerusalem. Peter and his political allies hoped that this reestablishment of the royal Davidic line would usher in a new era of Christianity based on the alternative Christian faith of his noble patrons, offsetting the corrupt institutional Church of Rome.[8]

In the Gringonneur deck, the Hermit has a long white beard and is wearing a hood. He is not carrying a lantern, as interpreted by the artists of later decks. He is actually holding an hourglass. The message and rallying cry of Peter the Hermit, ringing out from the steps of medieval cathedrals, was "It is time! It is time to liberate the Holy City where Christ was crucified and resurrected from the hands of the Saracens. It is time to restore the Holy Temple in Jerusalem." One thousand years had passed since the Romans had destroyed the Holy City and her Temple, scattering refugee Christians and Jews throughout the known world in Diaspora. It was time to restore the royal bloodline of King David— the *sang raal*—to the throne of Jerusalem.

The First Crusade of 1098-9 was successful, and Godfroi of Bouillion-Lorraine, a scion of the royal Merovingian line, was named the Liberator of Jerusalem. Within a few months he was dead, replaced on the throne by his brother Baudouin I. Descendants of their royal lineage have borne the title King of Jerusalem for nearly a thousand years as a result of the political action of the first Crusade. Although the title is empty of temporal power, its symbolic political influence is immense. The title "King of Jerusalem" is today inherited by descendants of the House of Habsburg-Lorraine, heirs to the imperial dynasty of the Holy Roman Empire and the throne of Austria-Hungary.

One substantial clue cries aloud the identity of the hermit. Appearing down the entire right side of the trump card is a rock formation, and, as every Christian knows, Peter's name means *rock*. Christ's words in the Gospel are taken very literally in Rome: "You are Peter, and upon this rock I will build my church." The people of Provence were steeped in the Gospels and the Word of God was their daily bread. It should not surprise us that elements from many significant Scripture passages should be the basis for the memory cards related to their unique version of the Christian faith.

STRENGTH

The next card is one of the most significant for the identification of the tarot trumps with the heresy of the *sang raal*—the blood royal brought by Mary Magdalene to the Mediterranean coast of France. In this enigmatic card, the virtue Strength is pictured, personified as a woman, holding in her arms a broken pillar.

In order to correctly understand this card, we must return to the pillars framing the door of Solomon's Temple, pillars named "Boaz" and "Jachin" (1 Kgs. 7:21). These pillars figure prominently in the lore of modern Freemasonry derived from roots in the medieval Order of the Knights of the Temple of Solomon (The Knights Templar), and they occur often among the catalogued watermarks of the heretics of the Grail. They are also found among the symbols carved during the Merovingian era into stone tablets in Metz to decorate the first Christian Church on French soil.

Figure 9 Pillars

Read together from right to left, the Hebrew words naming the two pillars mean "established in strength." The left pillar "Boaz" is translated directly "in strength," but it is also the name of the progenitor of King David, whose story is found in the Book of Ruth. Boaz was the second husband of the foreign widow Ruth, who accompanied her bereaved mother-in-law Naomi back to her homeland and there married her wealthy kinsman. Ruth and Boaz were the grandparents of Jesse, from whose "root" the savior was destined to spring (Is. 11:1). So the pillar named Boaz is associated with both the chosen family of the royal Davidic bloodline and its scriptural epithet "strength."

The identification of the Davidic bloodline with the virtue strength can be traced even further, all the way back to the Book of Genesis. This same family was also associated with the symbol of the Lion of Judah, a title given to Israel's kings based on lines from Genesis: "Judah, your brothers will praise you. . . your father's sons will bow down to you. You are a lion's cub, O Judah . . . the scepter shall not depart from Judah . . ." (Gn. 49:8-10). The Hebrew Scriptures state further that the princes of Israel shall be chosen from the tribe of Judah because he was the strongest of the twelve sons of Jacob, again equating the virtue of strength with the royal bloodline of Israel: "But of the tribe of Judah, who was the strongest among his brethren, came the princes" (1 Chr. 5:2).

The earliest mention of Jesus having descended in the royal bloodline of David is found in Paul's letter to the Romans, written in A.D. 57. In several places in the New Testament Gospels (written between A.D. 70-95), Jesus is said to be a descendant of David, and in the Book of Revelation 5:5 (dated A.D. 95-105), he is specifically called "the Lion of the tribe of Judah." The broken pillar on the Strength card refers to the broken legacy of the bloodline stemming from Boaz through Obed and Jesse to King David through the centuries down to Jesus and his heirs.

Drawing 3. "Strength" from the Mantegna deck

In several tarot decks the woman personifying Strength is pictured with a lion. Among the instructive cards mistakenly named for the Italian painter

Mantegna, two lions are embodied in her garments and a third stands near her; perhaps one lion for Judah, one for Boaz and one for Christ? Or they might represent past, present and future princes of the royal house of David. The figure seems to represent the epitome of the virtue—"thrice strong."

The twin pillars of the Temple of Solomon are said to have carved lily-work on their capitals (1 Kgs 7:19). This lily-work, visible in the broken pillar of the Strength trump, is the basis for the fleur-de-lis (flower of light) that is the universally recognized heraldic emblem for the Merovingians (450-750) and for the later royal dynasties of France. The other name for this emblem is the "little sword" and, as such, it serves as a visual reminder of the unique covenant of God with Israel that includes the rite of circumcision for all the sons of Sion. The stylized version of this symbol, ♠ , is replicated in the suit of spades found in modern card decks. This familiar symbol was originally a small sword.

A line still used in current Freemasonic rituals surrounding the myth of the Lost Word of the Master Mason is a poignant reminder of the alleged Messianic strength vested in the princely heirs of the Davidic bloodline of the tribe of Judah. The Masonic ritual states that until the "Lost Word" is found in a future age, "there is strength in the Lion of Judah, and he will prevail." This line seems particularly significant in light of the fact that the modern brotherhood of Freemasonry seems to be derived from the discredited and annihilated "Order of the Knights of the Temple of Solomon" by way of surviving members who fled to Scotland in 1307.

Figure 10. "Lion of Judah"

THE CHARIOTEER

The card that now follows, The Charioteer, seems again ill-named, for the knight pictured on the card in the Gringonneur deck is not driving a chariot. The conveyance he is riding looks more like a hearse, although the knight is dressed in armor and carrying a battle-ax. I believe that the warrior pictured is a member of the medieval order of the Knights of the Temple of Solomon returning from the Crusades. His one foot is standing on the letter "I" and the other shoe touches the letter "C" — "IC" being the Latin initials for Iesu Christi.

This card is, in my opinion, a direct reference to the rumor that the Knights of the Temple of Solomon discovered a great treasure concealed in the vaults under the Temple in Jerusalem, including archives containing secret information about Jesus. The Knights Templar are said to have brought this treasure back to Europe following their occupation of the Holy City, and their secrets are reported to have been of huge significance, powerful enough to discredit Roman Catholic doctrine. In Europe, rumors persist that the Knights of the Temple found written materials and perhaps even the grave or ossuary of Jesus, rumors that found expression centuries later in the symbol of the Freemasons, whose rituals and tenets sprang from Templar traditions: the grisly symbol of the skull and crossed bones. Modern Freemasonic initiation rites include reference to the excavation of the Temple archives and their transport to Europe by medieval knights. Whatever it was that they found, The Charioteer carries on its face the memory of Templar excavations of the Temple site in Jerusalem and the probable retrieval of certain relics or artifacts related to Jesus Christ.

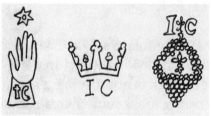

Figure 11. "IC" or Iesu Christi

An additional symbol of the Templar connection is illustrated on the trump's face. The cross is worn—not by the man in armor atop his unusual conveyance—but by the two horses pulling his conveyance. This was probably a safety measure, since the military clerics of the Order of the Knights Templar had been officially banned a century before the cards were painted. References to the Knights of the Temple and their legacy were politically incorrect in light of the brutal repression by the Inquisition.

The vehicle itself is also a bit of an anomaly, vaguely reminiscent of the curtained tabernacle that stands at the center of Roman Catholic altars. The tabernacle contains the ciborium, the chalice which holds the wafers of the Holy Eucharist, the "body and blood" of Jesus Christ. One of the greatest splits between Roman

Catholic teaching and the tenets of the heretics of the Grail developed over the dogma of Transubstantiation. Proclaimed at the Fourth Lateran Council in 1215, this theological statement insisted that only an ordained priest of the Roman Catholic Church was empowered to change ordinary bread and wine into the physical flesh and blood of Jesus Christ during the liturgy of the Mass.

Various sects of Christians preferred to see the presence of Christ on the altar as symbolic rather than physical. And they most surely denied the exclusive power of Rome's priests to produce the physical presence of Jesus on the altar during Mass, in spite of the numerous paintings depicting Saint Gregory's dream that attempted to popularize the doctrine. One such painting shows Christ standing stark naked on the altar, an all too literal illustration of the dogma. Since the heretics believed in a fully human Jesus, ancestor of their Merovingian friends, and may even have claimed to know the whereabouts of his earthly remains, it is natural to suppose that they viewed the claim of Transubstantiation with particular skepticism. Instead, they recognized the symbolic indwelling of the Holy Spirit in all things. Theirs was not a sacramental faith relying on priests and the rituals they performed or the doctrines they articulated to impart salvation. The heretics of the hidden church received the Gospel of Christ, not as a source of creeds to be memorized, but rather as a guide for a life to be lived. They honored Jesus as the "Way" and they called themselves Christians.

I believe the trump card called the Returning Templar (Charioteer) illustrates the "Great Secret" of the full humanity of Jesus in direct opposition to the orthodox doctrine of the bodily ascension of Jesus into heaven.

THE WHEEL OF FORTUNE

The card that follows in the traditional line-up of tarot trumps is called The Wheel of Fortune. This card has been lost from the Gringonneur deck, but in other decks it pictures a turn of the great Wheel of Fate, with people falling from it in wild disarray. The placement of this card seems logical, for the Templars expelled from the Middle East in 1291 soon incurred the jealous wrath of the French King Philip IV and of his ecclesiastic pawn, Pope Clement V. Within three decades of the failed final Crusade and the expulsion of Christians from the Levant and the Middle East, Philip and Clement orchestrated the arrest, torture, and execution of the members of the august Order of the Knights of the Temple of Solomon. This trump seems to be related to the swift turn of fate against the warrior-clerics who had amassed immense wealth and power over a period of two centuries. They were liquidated virtually overnight by the decree of Philip IV on October 13, 1307. The people of Europe were aghast at the "turn of the wheel" which tossed the Templars from a pinnacle of prestige to the depths of the French king's filthy dungeons. The date, Friday the thirteenth, lives in infamy— a grim and ominous reminder of the ignominious fate of the Templars.

JUSTICE

The next trump card bears an image of Justice, like Strength, personified as female, this time holding a sword and a set of scales, the typical aureola framing her face. The representation of the virtues of temperance, prudence, fortitude and justice as women is traditional in medieval art, and these figures are included among the instructional memory cards of the period. But here in the series of tarot trumps, the figure of Justice appears to have a touch of irony: "Vengence is mine, saith the Lord." The Inquisition spent seven years brutally torturing its political prisoners in an attempt to extract the details and hiding place of the reputed treasures of the Temple. The imprisoned members of the Order of the Templars were tried and sentenced by the inquisitors of the Roman establishment on exaggerated charges of blasphemy. It was a kangaroo court. The rigged proceedings dragged on, recorded in the annals of ecclesiastic judges who condemned many of the knights to be burned at the stake.

THE HANGED MAN

The judicial proceedings against the Knights of the Temple are further amplified on the following trump, number twelve, often declared the most enigmatic of the entire deck, The Hanged Man. He is, in fact, the tortured Templar. Stripped of honor, prestige and armor, the Templars were subjected to heinous tortures, including sexual tortures, supervised by the Inquisition.[9] The man in the picture is hanging by one leg, a metaphoric euphemism used in literature to represent the genitals. On this card, it is associated with the claims of the Merovingian bloodline, a fact illustrated in the position of the bent leg and exposed golden lining of the man's tunic. This awkward position of his leg forms a fleur-de-lis, the heraldic emblem of the Merovingian bloodline. The tortured Templar holds two bags of gold representing the monetary treasure of the suppressed order, as his leg and tunic represent the genealogical "family jewels" of the royal bloodline. His real treasure was "worth more than gold;" it included the revised Gospel of Christ and his Lady and the Great Secret of the *sang raal*.

Figure 12. Fleur-de-lis

DEATH

The card that follows, Death, depicts a skeleton with a scythe, the Grim Reaper, riding a black ass. Interestingly enough, the figures at his feet, trampled by his mount, are the very Pope and Emperor shown in two earlier trumps (numbered four and five). This Death card is tied directly to the suppression of the Knights of the Temple by a legend surrounding the death of the last Grand Master of the Order, Jacques de Molay, who together with his friend and fellow Templar, Geoffroi de Charnay, was roasted over charcoal in a slow and agonizing death in March, 1314, having somehow survived previous hideous tortures of the inquisitors. De Molay is claimed to have prophesied from the stake that both King Philip IV and Pope Clement V would meet him at the throne of God before the end of the year. And, in fact, both king and prelate died unexpectedly before the New Year, fulfilling the grisly prophecy of the martyred Grand Master. De Molay is one of the true heroes honored by modern freemasons as a forefather of their fraternity.

PRUDENCE

Now the story illustrated in the tarot trumps seems to shift gears. Another personified virtue, standard among the earlier memory cards, is pictured on the trump numbered fourteen; she is Prudence. She is seated, patiently pouring liquid from one container to another. She, too, is related to the stream of events in this visual flashcard catechism of the Grail heresy. The old containers of the heresy have now been destroyed. The citadels of the Templar families and former Cathar seminaries stand reduced to rubble and the songs of their troubadours are silenced. The waters of the Spirit and truth must be carefully transferred to new vessels in order to be preserved. Prudence requires that these new containers, "new wineskins," be carefully constructed and camouflaged to avoid the suspicions of the repressive establishment. These reliquaries of the heretical faith of the Grail church are now recognized in works of art, folklore, and certain artifacts of the Middle Ages: their watermarks, their unicorn tapestries, and the tarot itself.[10]

THE DEVIL

The card called The Devil follows. Depicted is an obscene figure of the masculine principle personified— the gross and repugnant bully of the Middle Ages— graphically expressed in his inelegant underwear. This brutal giant embodies the Inquisition. His big ears are trained to catch any hint of heresy, his chains designed to bind the hearts and minds of the people. He looms monstrous, ready to enslave the entire human race. The dutiful servants of this monster are the orthodox, carefully clearing his way, "lest he dash his foot upon a stone," a terrible parody of the temptation of Christ and the promise of temporal power HE refused when tempted (Mt. 4:5) but which the Church of Rome was eager to exercise.

THE TOWER

Perhaps the most obvious symbol of the heresy of the Holy Grail appears on the card that follows, The Tower, called the House of God in some later decks. The Tower has been stricken by the hand of God. The reference here is taken straight out of the Hebrew Psalm 89. The heirs of King David's royal house lament that God has forsaken his promises to them. For how long will God abandon his chosen one? His crown is in ashes, his citadels in ruins: "You have rejected and spurned . . . your anointed. You have renounced the covenant with your servant . . . You have broken down all his walls, you have laid his strongholds in ruins" (Ps. 89:39-41). Today, gazing on the ruined citadels of the Languedoc, one clearly senses this lamentation of the Davidic heirs in the rubble of the fortresses destroyed during the Albigensian Crusade and the later eradication of the Templar commanderies.

Of all the surviving pictures in the Gringonneur trumps, the Tower card is most closely linked to Mary Magdalene herself, for *magdala* in Hebrew means "tower" or "stronghold." The descendants of Israel's royal house, whose citadels were so ruthlessly demolished during the Albigensian Crusade, were rumored to have been descendants of Magdalene—the "vine of Mary"—as well as the *sang raal* of King David and of Christ.

Figure 13. Towers

In the book of Micah, the Hebrew prophet, we find a beautiful and poignant prophecy of Mary Magdalene's sad plight, a prophecy that uniquely bears her epithet, the "tower-stronghold":

> *As for you, O Magdal-eder (watchtower of the flock)*
> *O stronghold of the Daughter of Zion,*
> *the former dominion will be restored to you;*
> *Kingship will come to the Daughter of Jerusalem.*
> *Why do you now cry aloud—*
> *have you no king?*
> *Has your counselor perished,*
> *that pain seizes you like that of a woman in labor?*
> *Writhe in agony, O Daughter of Zion,*
> *like a woman in labor,*
> *for now you must leave the city*
> *and camp in the open field . . .*
> *And from there you shall be rescued.*
>
> (Mi. 4:8-10)

Intuition whispers that the epithet "Magdalene" applied to the "great Mary" of the Gospels was derived from this ancient prophetic passage that seems to apply to her own story as well as that of the people whom she represents as Queen. She, as well as Jerusalem, is identified with the "Widow Zion," abandoned by her Lord. And modern Freemasons, those unwitting guardians of the Grail secret, still call themselves "the widow's sons." The Book of Lamentations describes the plight of the desecrated city and the dark and distraught Lady Zion.

A very interesting and charming relief appears carved in a stone façade in the French city of Aix-en-Provence—once a Roman town. Neptune is depicted along with a "goddess" figure who bears on her head, instead of a crown, a replica of the walled city of which she is the patroness and protector. Anciently, the goddess is both guardian and representative of her city and her people. In fact, it appears that the jagged points of a monarch's crown are a stereotype derived from the ramparts of the city that once crowned the head of the goddess-patroness, much as the Acropolis honoring Athene crowns the hill above Athens. In ancient times, the Goddess was ruler, protector and servant of her people, the vessel of their wellbeing.

Perhaps in this context it is not hard to understand why the early Christian picked the Tower as an epithet for their First Lady. She represented the community as beloved of their Bridegroom. In fact, Mary Magdalene is equated very early in Church tradition with the woman who anointed Christ using precious nard from her alabaster jar, a reenactment of the nuptial rites of "sacred marriage" from the ancient cult of the "sacrificed Bridegroom-King" indigenous to the Near East.[11] In these *hieros gamos* liturgies, it was the prerogative of the royal bride, often a priestess surrogate of the Goddess, to choose and anoint her "Bridegroom-Messiah."

The Bride as a metaphor for the faith community is found throughout the Hebrew Bible, culminating in the ecstatic prophecy of Isaiah:

> *For Sion's sake I will not be silent*
> *until her vindication shines forth like*
> *the dawn . . .*
> *No longer shall you be called "forsaken"*
> *And your lands "abandoned,"*
> *But you shall be called "beloved"*
> *And your lands "espoused."*
>
> *(Is. 62:1-4)*

Rabbis understood the ancient metaphor of land and people as "Bride" and declared that the Song of Songs expressed the love of Yahweh for his people Israel. Rabbi Aqiba (d. 135) extolled the Song of Songs as the holiest of all the Scripture given to Israel, calling it the "Holy of Holies." Saint Paul and the early Christian fathers extended the same metaphor to the Church, the Bride whom Christ "loved so much, he gave his life for her" (Eph. 5:25). The author of Revelation uses the same metaphor when he prophesies the nuptials of the Christ, "the Lamb," and his beloved, the Holy City Jerusalem arrayed like a bride on her wedding day. For the early Christians, the woman who embodied the community as Bride was the Mary called the Magdalene, "the stronghold of the Daughter of Sion."

THE STAR

The card that followed The Tower has been lost from the Gringonneur deck, but in other decks is called The Star. In a fifteenth-century deck attributed to the artist

Antonio di Cicognara, a woman wearing a crown is holding a falcon on her left arm and holding a star in her right hand. Were these symbols the ones on the original trumps of the Gringonneur deck? The Star cards in later decks show a woman pouring liquid from two vessels into a stream, a sign of hope for the future, possibly bearing a veiled prophecy related to the astrological sign of Aquarius. Remembering the sacred vessels on the Prudence card used to preserve the waters of "spirit and truth" and elements of the Grail story, this card seems to prophesy that truth will be restored to the mainstream at some future time. Perhaps that time is now! The Star woman can be interpreted as a Water Carrier, the sign of the next age now dawning. There are two stars often used as symbols, each pregnant with meaning: the ☆, symbol for Venus, and the ✡, symbol for "sacred union" of the opposite energies.[12]

THE MOON

The next card, called The Moon, depicts two men drawing calculations on a parchment by the light of a crescent moon hanging in the night sky. The crescent moon is a well-known symbol for Islam, but also for the feminine or lunar principle. On this card it seems to be associated with the occult. These two men seem to be making furtive calculations from the stars, perhaps an astrological chart for a cathedral, so that it can be erected according to the principles of sacred geometry practiced by medieval masons. The men are holding instruments representing the V, or chalice, and the Λ, or blade, the archetypal symbols representing masculine and feminine. These same archetypal symbols for the polarities are carefully entwined in the compass and the T-square symbol of modern Freemasons. Careful balancing of the masculine and feminine principles is fundamental in architecture and in other sciences and arts. It is a reflection of the cosmic principle of equilibrium inherent in the "sacred union" or *hieros gamos* of the ancient civilizations. The ✡ is the "cosmic dance" of the opposite energies.

The rallying cry of the Crusaders was "Ave Millennium" rendered in symbol as △ , which is another "marriage" of the V and the Λ. This symbol is today taken to mean "Ave Maria," a further attempt at reclaiming the sacred feminine inherent in the symbol. For the medieval heretics of the Grail, the "Mary" hailed was the Bride. They were anticipating a millennium when their beloved *Domina* would be recognized and honored as partner of their Lord.

THE SUN

The Sun, like The Moon, is a card often found among the instructive memory decks compiled in the Middle Ages, innocuous in its familiarity. But on this next trump card, number nineteen, secret knowledge is conveyed. The woman holding the spindle is Briar Rose, the little princess in fairy-lore who pricked her finger and slept in seclusion for a hundred years. Or was it a thousand? Interesting, isn't it, that she was hidden away in a tower? How often in fairytale is the bride held captive in a remote tower stronghold? How often must the prince search for her in the face of tremendous obstacles and ordeals? Finally the handsome hero in the fairytale hacks his way through all the barriers in his path and finds his way to her tower room. There he awakens his Bride with a kiss.

The two previous cards, The Star and The Moon, illuminate the meaning of this card. Included among the "vessels" that preserved the waters of spirit and truth during the late Middle Ages were the occult sciences of alchemy and astrology, practiced under a cloak of darkness, by the light of the moon. But another protective vessel of suppressed truth was folktale, stories told in broad sunlight by day, and at the hearth by night, passed on from generation to generation of children gathered at their mothers' knees, right under the watchful eyes of the Inquisition. Who would bother to censor the silly songs and stories of children? Who would bother to silence their grandmothers, the wizened hags of fairytale? Here is found a vast reservoir of truth and wisdom! The people did not forget their little lost princess, the "sooty-faced" or "sleeping" bride so ubiquitous in folk- and fairy-lore.[13]

JUDGMENT DAY

Now comes the trump card called Judgment Day. Two angels with trumpets (again, the *trompes*!) are shown waking the dead, calling them forth from their graves. But those depicted are not the literally dead, nor is this a resurrection of the body on the last day of final judgment, a dogma of the Roman Catholic creed. These trumpets—like the *trompes* of the tarot—are those sent to awaken the human family that, figuratively speaking, has been buried alive for centuries! The clarion call of the trumpet breaks the silence of dawn: "Awake, O Sleeper!" These trumpets herald a new day of enlightenment and brother/sisterhood, a new millennium of joy and harmony. The song of the trumpets is "Reveille," not "Taps." The hands of the woman in the center foreground are signing an ancient invitation to enjoy the garden of the senses in human sexuality, a signal expressing the return of the feminine no longer repressed and vilified, but embraced as a fountain of delight and abundance. The trumpets on this card herald the New Millennium, the dawning era of Sacred Partnership.

THE WORLD

The twenty-second and final card, The World, shows the fulfillment of the ancient promise of peace on earth. The circle symbolizes perfection, and the seven hills encircled are symbolic of Rome, but by analogy also of the "Holy City" arrayed for her nuptials and for the entire family of God. The righteous ruler is pictured with crown, orb and scepter, symbolizing the eternal reign of God and the resulting Golden Age: "And a child shall lead them" (Is. 11:6). The hopeful tenets of the Grail heretics were not apocalyptic, but rather relied on the enlightened Christian community to recognize its role and responsibility as co-creator with God of a communal human destiny on this most sacred of created vessels—the planet Earth.

Ave Millennium!

SUMMARY

In these pages I have attempted to offer a scholarly interpretation of the symbols found in one of the earliest decks of playing cards containing the traditional tarot trumps. Attempts to link the tarot trumps to Egypt or India are purely speculative and not supported with hard evidence, that of our eyes. The earliest extant decks of cards are demonstrably European and medieval, painted by artists in a specific area—the northern provinces of Italy and southern France—the very cradle of the Grail legends, the troubadours and the Church of Love. Strong evidence that the trumps are a flashcard catechism for the heresy of the Grail is found in the watermarks from the pages of antique European Bibles and copies of such popular works as *The Song of Roland* and the *Romance of the Rose.* The most ardent desire of the heretics was to make copies of the Gospels available in the vernacular to all "believers" (*credants*) of the Languedoc. Theirs is a legacy of equality, enlightenment, and freedom from oppression, the very tenets of the Gospel they loved so well. It cannot be an accident that the watermarks, the tarot trumps, the troubadours and the Albigensian heresy all sprang from roots in Provence, where Mary Magdalene is claimed to have sought refuge from persecution in A.D. 42.

It may be natural to attempt to identify ancient archetypes in the cards that seem to be universal in character. But that does not affect the purely historical facts concerning the origins of the tarot trumps and their unique and intimate connection with the repressed secret of the Sacred Marriage at the heart of Christianity and the rumor of its ensuing bloodline of the Holy Grail. The "sacred union" of Jesus and Mary Magdalene

54

was the Great Secret of the Middle Ages. The power of this truth to split the Rock of Peter's Church was so feared by the Roman hierarchy that ruthless tactics were employed to suppress it. Like a sturdy vine, it somehow survived in the art and artifacts of medieval Europe, and "in spite of dungeon, fire, and sword" it flourishes still!

Stone tablet from "Saint Peter to the Nuns," Metz

NOTES

Chapter I

1. Brian Innes, *The Tarot: How to Use and Interpret the Cards* (New York: Crescent Books, 1987. First published London: Macdonald & Co., Ltd., 1976), 4.

2. Margaret Starbird, *The Woman with the Alabaster Jar: Mary Magdalen and the Holy Grail* (Santa Fe, NM: Bear & Company, 1993), 59-62.

3. Michael Baigent, Richard Leigh and Henry Lincoln, *Holy Blood, Holy Grail* (New York: Dell Publishing Co., 1983). First published as *The Holy Blood and the Holy Grail* (London: Jonathan Cape, Ltd., 1982), 139. René d'Anjou (1408-1480), heir to the House of Lorraine, was allegedly a close friend of the Sforza family of Milan. For interesting background about the Visconti family in Milan, please see Barbara Tuchman, *A Distant Mirror* (New York: Ballantine Books, 1978).

4. The sketches of medieval watermarks sprinkled throughout the text are derived from those found in Charles-Moïse Briquet, *Les Filigranes*. Edited by Allan Stevenson. In *The New Briquet, Jubilee Edition*, general ed. J.S.G. Simmons (Amsterdam: The Paper Publications Society, 1968) vol. iii, iv.

5. Henry Lincoln, *The Holy Place* (New York: Brown & Little, Arcade Books, 1991), 59-60.

6. Margaret Starbird, *The Goddess in the Gospels: Reclaiming the Sacred Feminine* (Santa Fe, NM: Bear & Company, 1998) 128.

7. Harold Bayley, *The Lost Language of Symbolism* (Totowa, NJ: Rowman and Littlefield, 1974) ii, 93.

8. Starbird, *The Goddess in the Gospels, op.cit.* Appendix 3, 158-9. The *gematria* of "the Magdalene" (Greek: *h*

Magdalhnh) is directly related to the Vesica Piscis, the $()$, an ancient symbol for the Great Goddess.

Chapter II

1. Innes, *op.cit., 10.*
2. Innes, *ibid.*
3. Stuart R. Kaplan, *The Encyclopedia of Tarot* (Stanford, CT: U.S. Games Systems, Inc., 1978), 111.
4. Starbird, *The Woman with the Alabaster Jar, op. cit.* 104-16.

Chapter III

1. Richard Cavendish, *The Tarot* (New York: Crescent Books, 1975), 17.
2. Bayley, *The Lost Language of Symbolism, op.cit., ii,* 319-320.
3. Harold Bayley, *New Light on the Renaissance* (New York: B. Blom, 1967). Bayley provides an in-depth discussion of the spread of the heresy by the travelling troubadours and jugglers of the High Middle Ages.
4. Bayley, *The Lost Language of Symbolism, op. cit.* 320-21.
5. "The Gospel of Philip" in James Robinson, ed., *The Nag Hammadi Library: In English* (San Francisco: Harper & Row, 1981), 135-36.
6. Bayley, *The Lost Language of Symbolism, op. cit.,* 26. See also Starbird, *The Woman with the Alabaster Jar, op. cit.,* 124, 29-131, for more detailed discussion of heretics' use of the red X as a symbol for truth and enlightenment— the "other" Christianity.
7. See Starbird, *The Goddess in the Gospels, op. cit.* 140-41 and 159-60, for thorough discussion of the *gematria* of Mary Magdalene's name and its implications for her relationship

with Christ and their connection with the Zodiac sign of
"Pisces"—The Fishes. This discussion is derived from
the ancient canon of sacred geometry described in the
work of John Michell, *The Dimensions of Paradise* (San
Francisco: Harper & Row, 1989), and David Fideler,
Jesus Christ, Sun of God (Wheaton, IL: Quest Books,
1993).

8. See Baigent, *op.cit.*, 111-16, for detailed discussion of
the political objectives of the First Crusade.

9. See Peter Tompkins, *The Magic of Obelisks* (New York:
Harper & Row, 1981), 61-2, for graphic discription and
illustration of the tortured Templars.

10. See Starbird, *The Woman with the Alabaster Jar, op. cit.*
chapters 5-7, for detailed discussion of the medieval art
and artifacts related to the heresy of the Holy Grail.

11. *Ibid.*, 27-31.

12. See Henry Lincoln, *The Holy Place, op.cit.*, 125-29, for
a fascinating study of the sacred geometry linking the
two stars in the area surrounding the village Rennes-le-
Chateau in France.

13. See Starbird, *The Woman with the Alabaster Jar, op. cit.*
145-55, for further discussion of the lost bride in
European folk- and fairytale.

GLOSSARY

Albigensian Crusade

Crusade mounted by French King and Pope to suppress heresy in southern France. War, raging from 1209-1250, devastated the area and its culture.

Athene

Greek Goddess of Wisdom, patroness of Athens.

Bempo Deck

Painted tarot cards dated 1484. Trumps were probably copied from the earlier Gringonneur deck.

Boaz

Second husband of Ruth in the Hebrew Bible. His name means "strength." Name of the left-hand pillar of the Temple of Solomon in Jerusalem.

Charles VI Deck

Same as Gringonneur Deck.

Fleur-de-lis

Heraldic device of the Merovingian kings known as the "little sword." Now the symbol for France.

Freemasonry

Fraternal society officially formed in the eighteenth century based on roots in the

"Order of the Knights of the Temple of Solomon." Rites of modern freemasons retain elements reflecting their medieval origins.

Gematria

Number codes widely used by Greek and Hebrew philosophers based on the numeric values of the letters of their alphabets. The system predates Plato and is practiced extensively in the writings of the New Testament (Greek Bible).

Gringonneur Deck

Same as Charles VI deck, now determined to be a later deck, possibly of northern Italian origin rather than the one attributed to the painter Gringonneur mentioned in records of the French king in 1392. Probably painted 1425-1450. Sixteen trumps and one face card survive, displayed in the Bibliotèque Nationale in Paris.

Hermes

Greek god, "messenger of the gods"—the "trickster" and bringer of enlightenment through synchronicity. Identified with Egyptian

"Thoth" and Christian "Holy Spirit."

ICHTHYS

Greek for "fish." The acronym abbreviates the phrase "Jesus Christ, Son of God, Savior," identifies Christ as the "fish."

Inquisition

The Holy Office charged with defending the purity of the Roman Catholic doctrines of faith. Formed in 1233 in France to suppress the Albigensian heresies.

Jachin

The right-hand pillar of the Temple of Solomon in Jerusalem. One of the "twin pillars." See "Boaz."

Judah

Son of Jacob, the patriarch. Princes of Israel were chosen from the tribe of Judah because of their strength.

Levant

"Land of the rising sun." The Middle Eastern lands bordering the Mediterranean east and south of Greece. Christians built and occupied citadels and settlements in this area from 1099-1291, when they were expelled by the Saracens.

Magdala	Hebrew word meaning "watchtower," "stronghold," "citadel." New Testament epithet of Mary "the Magdalene" was probably derived from this word.
H Magdalhnh	Greek spelling of the epithet for Mary Magdalene.
Merovingian dynasty	Frankish kings from fifth to the eighth century. Last Merovingian king was deposed by Pepin, the father of Charlemagne. Bloodline survived and flourished in noble families of Europe. Legends maintain descent from Mary Magdalene — "the Vine of Mary."
Moors	Muslim Arabs who conquered and then occupied northern Africa, Spain and the Mediterranean coast of France from eighth to the fourteenth century.
Order of the Knights of the Temple of Solomon	Chivalric order founded in 1118 to protect pilgrims in the Holy Land. Allegedly these knights excavated the Temple treasury. Order liquidated in 1307 under charge

of blasphemy, members were tortured and exterminated in France. Some fled and survived in other countries.

Ossuary

A box, usually ornate, used to store skeletal remains, often of an important person. Jews kept the remains of their kings in ossuaries.

Pisces

Latin for "The Fishes," the rising sign of the Zodiac at the time of Christ. After 2000 years, the Age of Pisces is soon to be replaced by the Age of Aquarius.

Sangraal

Old French word often translated "Holy Grail." When divided *sang raal*, it means "blood royal," believed to refer to the royal Davidic bloodline of the heirs of Jesus and Mary Magdalene.

Sophia

Wisdom archetype in Hellenistic tradition. Honored in the Gnostic gospels as the "sacred feminine."

Tarot

Card decks of medieval design and later copies;

word is derived from Italian *tarocchi*.

Tarot trumps   Series of 22 playing cards with pictures of various archetypes and images related to the medieval heresy of the Holy Grail.

Templars   See "Order of Knights of the Temple of Solomon."

Transubstantiation   Doctrine of the Roman Catholic Church proclaimed in 1215. States that bread and wine are physically changed into the actual body and blood of Jesus by a priest during the liturgy of the Mass.

Visconti-Sforza Decks   Several decks of Tarot cards belonging to the ruling familes of Milan painted in the mid-fifteenth century contained series of 22 trumps. Many cards from these decks survive in various museums and libraries.

Watermarks (heretical)   Marks manufactured into sheets of paper. Fossils of the alternative Christian faith

found embossed in paper of
Bibles and other works in
medieval Europe (1280-
1600).

CHRONOLOGY

B.C.E   **(Before Christian Era—B.C.)**

1000   King David

970-950   King Solomon, son of David, rules Israel, builds the first Temple in Jerusalem.

586   Solomon's Temple is destroyed by Nebuchadnezzar; Jews exile in Babylon begins.

580-500   Pythagoras (d. 497). Greek mathematicians/ philosophers establish "canon of sacred number" reflecting cosmology of the ancient world.

520   Jews return to Jerusalem. Inspired by the prophet Haggai, they begin to rebuild the city and temple.

427-347   Plato, Greek philosopher and initiate of the school of Pythagoras, uses *gematria* in his *Laws* and *Timaeus*.

384-322   Aristotle

333-330   The Middle East is conquered by armies of Alexander the Great.

330-63   Greeks establish hegemony over Israel, Egypt and surrounding Middle Eastern Countries.

167   Judas Maccabeus leads rebellion against foreign rulers in Judea; Jewish "Hasmonian"dynasty established.

63   Pompey lays siege to Jerusalem; Romans have hegemony in Israel.

100-44   Julius Caesar, soldier, is emperor of Rome.

40-4   King Herod the Great rules Judea, destroys the second Temple and builds "Herod's Temple" on the Temple Mount; allied with Rome.

7-3   Birth of Jesus Christ

C.E.   **(Common Era—A.D.)**

30-33   Approximate dates of the ministry and crucifixion of Jesus.

26-36   Pontius Pilate serves as Roman Procurator (governor) of Judea.

42   Persecution of Christians in Judea forces Mary Magdalene and her family and friends to flee to Gaul (French legend).

50-67   Letters of Saint Paul (d. 67) are written to cities of the Roman Empire.

66-73   Romans put down rebellion in Judea.

67-70   Dead Sea Scrolls in earthen jars are concealed in caves near Qumran.

70   Roman legions destroy Jerusalem and Herod's Temple.

70   Traditional date of the Gospel of Mark, which is written in Rome.

73	Masada, last Jewish stronghold in Judea, falls to Roman army.
80-85	Gospel of Matthew is written, probably in Alexandria.
85	Gospel of Luke is written.
90-95	Gospel of John is understood to have been written in this time.
95	Consensus date is understood for the Book of Revelation (Apocalypse of John).
50-300	Christians are persecuted in the Roman Empire.
325	Council of Nicaea, Emperor Constantine makes Christianity official religion of the Roman Empire.
325-400	Persecution of unorthodox sects, Gnostic Christianity; Gnostic texts are concealed in earthen jars at Nag Hammadi, Egypt c. 400.
340-420	Saint Jerome, translator of the Bible into the "vulgate" (people's) Latin
354-430	Augustine is Bishop of Hippo.
410-476	Various barbarian tribes sweep across western Europe, sack Rome; the empire falls.
428-751	Merovingian dynasty rules the Franks in Gaul (France).
481-511	Reign of Merovingian King Clovis I; he converts France to Roman Christianity (496)

c. 635-711   Muslims expand and conquor northern Africa, Spain, and southern France.

732   Charles Martel (d. 741) defeats the Moors at Battle of Tours (Poitiers), prevents further invasion of Western Europe by Muslims.

754-768   Pepin rules the Franks, deposes the last Merovingian king.

768-814   Charlemagne, son of Pepin, rules the Franks. He is crowned Holy Roman Emperor by Pope Leo in Rome, Christmas, 800.

c. 810-885   Norsemen terrorize coastal areas of Europe.

1066   William the Norman (the Conqueror) conquers England at the Battle of Hastings.

1050-1250   Cathar heresy spreads across northern Italy and in the Languedoc, southern France.

1098-1099   First Crusade. Christian Crusaders plan to take Jerusalem from the Saracens and establish a Christian Kingdom in Israel.

1099   Godfroi of Boullion conquers Jerusalem and is given the title "Protector of Jerusalem."

1118   Order of the Knights of the Temple of Solomon is established to protect pilgrims in the Holy land. Excavate under the Temple.

1209-1250   Brutal Albigensian Crusade is waged by Pope and French King against the heretics in southern France.

1215	Fourth Lateran Council establishes the doctrine of Roman Catholic Doctrine of Transubstantiation.
1224-1274	Life of Thomas Aquinas, author of the *Summa Theologica*.
1233	Inquisition is established to protect the faith, punish heretics.
1244	Montsegur, citadel seminary of the Cathars, falls after siege.
1291	Crusaders and Christians are expelled from the Holy Land.
1307	Templar Order is liquidated by decree of Philip IV on charges of heresy.
1314	Jacques de Molay, last Grand Master of the Templars, is burned; King Philip IV and Pope Clement V also die before year's end.
1350	Playing cards are first mentioned in a written text in Europe.
1392	Three hand-painted card decks are ordered for the amusement of French king Charles VI.
1412-1431	Joan of Arc defeats England's armies, has Charles VII crowned.
1420-1450	Gringonneur (Charles VI) tarot deck is painted; 16 trump and one court card survive.
1440-1485	Several card decks are painted for the ducal families of Milan—the so-called Visconti-Sforza decks.

SELECTED BIBLIOGRAPHY

Baigent, Michael, Richard Leigh and Henry Lincoln. *The Holy Blood and the Holy Grail*. London: Jonathan Cape, Ltd., 1982. Reprinted as *Holy Blood, Holy Grail*, New York: Dell Publishing Co., 1983.

Bayley, Harold. *The Lost Language of Symbolism*. Totowa, NJ: Rowman and Littlefield, 1974. First published Great Britain: Williams and Norgate, 1912.

_____. *New Light on the Renaissance Displayed in Contemporary Emblems*. London: J.M. Dent, 1909. Republished New York: B. Blom, 1967.

Briquet, Charles-Moïse. *Les Filigranes*. Edited by Allan Stevenson. In *The New Briquet Jubilee Edition*, general ed. J.S.G. Simmons. Amsterdam: The Paper Publications Society, 1968.

Cavendish, Richard. *The Tarot*. London: M. Joseph, Ltd., 1975. Reprinted New York: Crescent Books, 1986.

Innes, Brian. *The Tarot: How to Use and Interpret the Cards*. New York: Crescent Books, 1987. First published London: Macdonald & Co., Ltd., 1976.

Kaplan, Stuart R. *The Encyclopedia of Tarot*. Stanford, CT: U.S. Games Systems, Inc., 1978.

Lincoln, Henry. *The Holy Place*. New York: Brown &

Little, Arcade Books, 1991.

Robinson, James. M., ed. *The Nag Hammadi Library: In English.* New York: Harper & Row, 1981. First Published Leiden, The Netherlands: E. J. Brill, 1978.

Russell, Douglas A. *Costume History and Style.* New Jersey: Prentice-Hall, Inc., 1983.

Starbird, Margaret. *The Goddess in the Gospels: Reclaiming the Sacred Feminine.* Santa Fe, NM: Bear & Company, 1998.

_____. *The Woman with the Alabaster Jar: Mary Magdalen and the Holy Grail.* Santa Fe, NM: Bear & Company, 1993.

Tompkins, Peter. *The Magic of Obelisks.* New York: Harper & Row, Publishers, 1981.

Tuchman, Barbara W. *A Distant Mirror.* New York: Ballantine Books, 1978.

Wilcox, R. Turner. *The Mode in Hats and Headdress.* New York: Charles Scribner's Sons, 1959.

ABOUT THE AUTHOR

For several years as a teenager and military dependent, Margaret Starbird lived in Bamberg, Germany. She traveled widely in Europe and later studied comparative literature and European history with an emphasis on medieval studies at the University of Maryland. In 1963-4 she studied on an educational Fulbright Grant at the Christian Albrechts Universität, in Kiel, Germany, and in 1966 she completed a master of arts degree at the University of Maryland, where she continued to teach German language and literature classes as an instructor until 1968. Twenty years later she enrolled as a student at Vanderbilt Divinity School in Nashville, Tennessee, where she pursued her passionate interest in her Judeo-Christian heritage and scriptures. She taught religious education and scripture studies for Roman Catholics for many years, and now gives frequent lectures and retreats centered on the restoration of the Sacred Feminine in Christianity.

Starbird is the author of *The Woman with the Alabaster Jar: Mary Magdalen and the Holy Grail* and *The Goddess in the Gospels: Reclaiming the Sacred Feminine*, both centered on the theme of the lost Bride in the Christian story and the medieval heresy of the Holy Grail. One of the significant artifacts associated with this heresy is the tarot, the subject of her current book.

Starbird is a wife and mother of five children, now grown. She and her husband, a retired army officer, currently reside in the Pacific Northwest.

Margaret Starbird can be reached through her website:
http://www.telisphere.com/~starbird

or by mail:

Margaret Starbird
P.O. Box 97043
Lakewood, WA 98497-0043

To order please send check or money order to the
above address.

*The Tarot Trumps and the Holy Grail: Great Secrets of the
Middle Ages*
$15.00 + $3.00 shipping and handling

*The Goddess in the Gospels: Reclaiming the Sacred
Feminine*
$15.00 + $3.00 shipping and handling

This book has been self-published by Margaret Starbird with
technical support of the editorial staff of WovenWord Press.